GOOD OMENS

TAROT DECK GUIDEBOOK

WRITTEN BY
Minerva Siegel

ILLUSTRATED BY
Lúthien Leerghast

TITAN
BOOKS
London

CONTENTS

INTRODUCTION 05

**UNDERSTANDING
YOUR TAROT DECK** 07

MAJOR ARCANA 11
THE FOOL 12
I THE MAGICIAN 15
II THE HIGH PRIESTESS 16
III THE EMPRESS 19
IV THE EMPEROR 20
V THE HIEROPHANT 23
VI THE DUO 24
VII THE CHARIOT 27
VIII STRENGTH 28
IX THE HERMIT 31
X THE WHEEL OF FORTUNE 32
XI JUSTICE 35
XII THE HANGED MAN 36
XIII DEATH 39
XIV TEMPERANCE 40
XV THE DEVIL 43
XVI THE TOWER 44

XVII THE STAR	47
XVIII THE MOON	48
XIX THE SUN	51
XX JUDGMENT	52
XXI THE WORLD	55

MINOR ARCANA	**57**
SUIT OF ANGELS	58
SUIT OF VESSELS	72
SUIT OF DEMONS	86
SUIT OF HUMANS	100

TAROT READINGS	**115**
CARING FOR YOUR DECK	117
PREPARING TO READ TAROT	119
THE INEFFABLE PLAN	120
THE DOCTOR'S QUANDARY	122
GABRIEL'S SELF-DISCOVERY	124

ABOUT THE AUTHOR	126
ABOUT THE ILLUSTRATOR	127

INTRODUCTION

Are you curious about your fate? Wondering what your future holds? Don't wait 'til doomsday to find out what's in store for you! Come, angels, demons, humans, and witches alike! Allow the sly serpent Crowley to tempt you into discovering the ins and outs of your future and fortune using this miraculous Good Omens tarot deck and guidebook. Who knows what mysteries, marvels, truths, and trickeries will be revealed when you sit down to shuffle these illuminating cards?

The age-old conflict between good and evil has never been more fraught with peril and excitement. What's your role in this battle? Your past, present, and future will become as clear as the Ritz's crystal champagne flutes with the help of friends and foes, including angels Muriel, Uriel, Saraqael, and Sandalphon and wicked hellions like Beelzebub and Shax. You'll learn to follow your heart with the archangel Aziraphale, welcome fast-paced change with the devilish Crowley and his iconic 1926 Bentley, and open your heart to new beginnings with Nina, the barista extraordinaire. So, whatever are you waiting for? A sign from Agnes Nutter herself? Let's get to it!

UNDERSTANDING YOUR TAROT DECK

The idea of learning to read tarot may seem daunting at first, but it's really quite easy when you get the hang of it. There are seventy-eight tarot cards in a deck, and each one has a different meaning depending on whether it's drawn upright or reversed. The first twenty-two cards are called the Major Arcana. They represent important themes and major life lessons with lasting impact. Numbered zero through XXI, they chronologically tell the story of the Fool (the first card in the Major Arcana), a figure who goes on a marvelous adventure that's both hellishly harrowing and heartwarming in equal measure. He encounters a broad variety of situations, predicaments, highs, and lows that may feel reminiscent of events in your own life. On this journey, he also meets personality archetypes that fall across the whole spectrum of good and evil. Navigating these challenges and figures ultimately leads to personal growth, enlightenment, and fulfillment.

The rest of the tarot cards in the deck are called the Minor Arcana. Representing everyday situations and themes with short-term effects, the fifty-six Minor Arcana cards are sorted into four suits. In this deck, the four suits are Angels, Vessels, Demons, and Humans. They represent the traditional tarot suits of Wands, Cups, Swords, and Pentacles, respectively.

The suit of Angels is associated with creativity, passion, and inspiration. It corresponds to the element of fire.

The suit of Vessels deals with emotions, romantic relationships, and personal connections with family or friends. It corresponds to the element of water.

The suit of Demons represents ambition, conflicts, and our relationship with power. It corresponds to the element of air.

The suit of Humans explores the physical world and our relationship to it, including aspects of life such as careers, finances, material possessions, and the home. It corresponds to the element of earth.

Each of these suits contains four court cards: King, Queen, Knight, and Page. They symbolize personality types, behavior patterns, and sometimes actual people in your life. The remaining cards are numbered I (Ace) through X.

MAJOR ARCANA

THE FOOL

The Fool represents someone heading out on a new adventure, like Adam Young. Though Adam's inexperience may lead to missteps (like summoning the Four Horsemen of the Apocalypse while ignoring friends' desperate pleas to not bring about the end of the world), the journey he goes on is transformative and fulfilling in the end.

UPRIGHT: You're beginning what is destined to be a life-changing journey of self-actualization, full of twists and turns (and perhaps even angels and demons), ultimately culminating in personal growth. Indulge your sense of adventure by jumping into this new venture with enthusiasm.

REVERSED: Are you taking more risks than are necessary? Reversed, the Fool suggests you may be acting impulsively. Take the conspiracy theories you read in the *New Aquarian* with a grain of salt and listen to your friends. If they try to offer you a healthier, more balanced perspective, trust that they're acting in your best interests.

I · THE MAGICIAN

The Magician is a crafty, motivated manifestation master like the marvelously multitalented medium Madame Tracy.

UPRIGHT: The Magician is an action-oriented person who uses their innate talents to create the life they want to live. This tarot card is a signal to embrace your skills and natural aptitudes, however unconventional they may be, and put them to work for you. If you stay authentic and passionate, you'll attract success like a magnet.

REVERSED: When reversed, the Magician suggests you're not making the most of your potential. You may be hiding your talents, or perhaps you just haven't fully discovered and embraced them yet. Open yourself up to new opportunities and follow your passions. If you stay open-minded, you may just find yourself in a miraculous situation that will reveal your most important talent (whether that's mediumship or something a bit more conventional).

II · THE HIGH PRIESTESS

The High Priestess is a wise, intuitive, spiritual figure like Agnes Nutter, author of *The Nice and Accurate Prophecies of Agnes Nutter, Witch*.

UPRIGHT: The High Priestess encourages you to connect with your intuition. While you may or may not be spiritually privy to otherworldly information that will ultimately prevent an apocalypse, what is certain is that the answers you're seeking are inside of you. Be still, block out the noise and chaos of the physical world, and tune in to your gut feelings. They won't steer you wrong.

REVERSED: Your intuition is calling to you, but you're ignoring it. Remember, it's there to help you! Get back into alignment with your destiny by removing your head from the sand and acknowledging the need to check in with yourself. Reconnecting with your intuition and spiritual needs will help you move forward in the right direction.

III · THE EMPRESS

The Empress is a maternal, nurturing figure—much like Deirdre Young, mother to Adam Young (aka the Antichrist himself).

UPRIGHT: Kindness, caretaking, and nurturing are your top priorities now. This could mean caring for yourself or for others who are depending on you. Cultivate beauty in your life by tending to your garden or redecorating your home. You'll feel more balanced if your living spaces bring you genuine comfort and joy.

REVERSED: Reversed, this tarot card encourages you to make time to stop and enjoy the little things. You've been too caught up in the hustle and bustle of everyday life to enjoy the beauty and comfort around you. Take a walk, smell the flowers, and enjoy the warm sunshine. Reconnecting with nature and beauty will give you the refreshing pause you need to love life again.

IV · THE EMPEROR

Like the archangel Gabriel, the Emperor is a respected, patriarchal authority figure who expects the best from those around him.

UPRIGHT: The Emperor doesn't have time or patience for whimsy and freethinking angels. This card advises you to stay disciplined and stick to tried-and-true methods to get the job done. Nonconformity and deviating from the set path will only lead to trouble now. Stay focused on the Great Plan!

REVERSED: Kidnap any angels lately? Reversed, the Emperor suggests you're abusing your powerful position. Don't let your ego get the better of you. Reassess your relationship with authority to find better balance. People are counting on you to be fair and just.

V · THE HIEROPHANT

The Chattering Order of St. Beryl is an institution that respects hierarchies and tradition, as does the Hierophant.

UPRIGHT: It's time to listen and learn from those with more experience than you. Whether at work, at school, or in a satanic convent, you're perfectly positioned to soak up valuable knowledge and lessons that will be crucial to you as you progress through life. Pay attention and make the most of this opportunity, or it may just go up in flames.

REVERSED: Sometimes stepping out of line and doing things your own way is the best policy. When reversed, the Hierophant advises that this is one of those times. Break free from rigid restrictions and follow your own path. You are your own guide now, and you'll have everything you need to succeed by listening to your own advice rather than anyone else's.

VI · THE DUO

Well, isn't this just tickety-boo? The Duo card represents a harmonious, wonderful, mutually beneficial union, much like the relationship between Crowley and Aziraphale.

UPRIGHT: You're glowing! You've made a marvelous, miraculous connection with someone. Things feel—dare you say—magical. Whether this connection is a close friendship or romantic relationship, it's clear that destiny has brought you together. The Duo card also carries with it an element of choice. Will you choose to stay in this heavenly partnership despite any and all hellish complications? Or will you give in and let outside forces succeed in driving you apart?

REVERSED: A once-heavenly connection has crashed back down to earth. You're feeling out of step with someone who means a great deal to you, and you're wondering whether patching things up is worth the effort. Perhaps you have simply grown apart. After all, some people just aren't meant to stay in your life forever. A bit of soul-searching will reveal whether you should double down on your efforts and recommit to this person or move on.

VII · THE CHARIOT

The Chariot represents momentum, action, and taking ownership of your own destiny, like Adam Young does as he pedals off to Tadfield Air Base. This event culminates in a confrontation with his father, Satan, and averts Armageddon.

UPRIGHT: It's time to pick up the pace! You're on a mission, and things are moving quickly now. Whether you're rushing off with friends to Tadfield Air Base to confront your destiny or taking measurable action with slightly less potential for global catastrophe, the Chariot advises you to stay focused. The potential for real progress is there if you stay motivated.

REVERSED: If you're feeling like you've lost control, it may be that you're just trying to control the uncontrollable. You're most comfortable when you're in control, but the fact is that life can be, well, *ineffable*. Sometimes destiny and fate have plans that differ from your own. Relax, take a step back, and see how things play out without trying to exert power over the situation.

VIII · STRENGTH

The Strength card represents compassionate leadership, bravery, and inner strength—all traits Adam Young demonstrates when he confronts his father, the one and only Satan himself, to stop Armageddon.

UPRIGHT: You won't win this fight with brawn and might. Like the antichrist, you'll have to use kindness, cleverness, and inner strength to save the day. Strength comes in many forms; you don't have to be the biggest, strongest, or baddest to come away victorious. There's power in radical softness, too.

REVERSED: If you're feeling weak, powerless, and disregarded, don't despair. Strength, when reversed, reminds you that you're more influential and capable than you currently believe yourself to be. Don't look for validation and affirmation from outside sources. Praise your own accomplishments to reconnect with your self-confidence. Remember how far you've come and how many tricky obstacles you've cleverly fought your way through. You're stronger than you're giving yourself credit for.

IX · THE HERMIT

The Hermit is a solitary figure who likes to do things his own way and answer to no one—like the inimitable demon Crowley.

UPRIGHT: It's time to take a leaf out of Crowley's book. Go back to your brutalist lair and enjoy your own solitary company. The Hermit advises you to make time for reflection and rumination. Stop to take stock of the situation you find yourself in rather than acting impulsively or going through life on autopilot. Some quality time spent with the number one person in your life (yourself) will benefit you immeasurably.

REVERSED: Alright, you've been alone too long. You may be going a bit stir-crazy. It's time to get out and rejoin the hustle and bustle of the real world before you start brutalizing your poor houseplants. Call up a longtime companion for a sushi date or meet up with pals at your favorite coffee shop. Shake off your doldrums by getting out of the house and throwing yourself into the world again.

X · THE WHEEL OF FORTUNE

Even the best-laid plans (and the best-drawn chalk circles) are subject to the whims of fate. The Wheel of Fortune represents divine destiny and unexpected change.

UPRIGHT: The Wheel of Fortune is an ineffable force unmoved by the hopes, pleas, and perils of man. When things are going well, enjoy them, because they won't go well forever. Eventually, your fortune will shift, and you'll find yourself in an unlucky position—as when Aziraphale accidentally steps backward into the still-charged portal beneath his bookshop rug and is unwittingly transported back to heaven. Accept the cyclical nature of luck and fortune. Enjoy the highs and don't despair during the lows.

REVERSED: Oh, bugger. Reversed, the Wheel of Fortune represents bad luck and unfavorable developments. If you've pulled this reversed card in a tarot reading asking about an outcome, it is a clearly negative response. Things won't go in your favor. However, don't despair! Sometimes things that seem negative at first wind up being positive events in the grand scheme of things. So take this card with a grain of salt and put your trust in the ineffable plan.

XI · JUSTICE

Just as Thou-Shalt-Not-Commit-Adultery Pulsifer leads an angry mob of townsfolk to the cottage of Agnes Nutter to set her ablaze for her witchery, Justice represents cause and consequence.

UPRIGHT: Every action has a consequence. Sometimes even the most well-intentioned witches find themselves in hot water. Avoid regret by taking the time to think through your actions. Carefully consider any possible developments you may set into motion. Above all, prioritize treating others with fairness and respect.

REVERSED: Beware rushing into hasty judgments. Make sure you have all the facts and understand the situation fully before setting an angry mob on someone. You might feel as though you have enough information to proceed with condemnation or absolution, but Justice, when reversed, suggests that you step back and take another look at the facts. Consider seeking the opinion of an uninvested third party to get an impartial perspective on the matter before taking action.

XII · THE HANGED MAN

The Hanged Man is someone who's found himself caught in an unexpected moment of pause, like the wicked Hastur when Crowley imprisons him in the answering machine.

UPRIGHT: An unplanned delay or setback leads to a suspended pause. Use this to your benefit. Take advantage of the situation by seeing things from a different perspective. Look around and you'll find beneficial new avenues you might have missed if you were too caught up in your momentum. Embrace the delay.

REVERSED: You're feeling as trapped as Hastur in cunning Crowley's answering machine. Wriggle though you might, you won't worm your way out of this until you calm down and have a good think. Things may not be quite as hopeless as they seem right now; you can overcome obstacles with ingenuity and good timing. Consider your options, wait for the right moment, and make your move.

XIII · DEATH

Death represents major transitions and transformations. What looks like an ending could end up being a new beginning.

UPRIGHT: Transformation is an essential condition of life. None of us stay the same forever; we're always in a state of change—physically, emotionally, and otherwise. Embrace this important period in your life. Change can sometimes be daunting, but it can also lead you to exciting new adventures. This card serves as a reminder that endings often make room for new growth.

REVERSED: There's no use in digging in your heels to avoid an inevitable ending. A chapter in your life should have closed by now, but you may be stubbornly refusing to turn the page. Reversed, Death advises that there's no sense in that. Change is inevitable, and delaying it is only prolonging your anxiety. It's time to let go and move on into the future.

XIV · TEMPERANCE

Nanny Ashtoreth seeks to tempt Warlock Dowling into embracing evil, while Brother Francis aims to influence him into compassion and kindness. Their goal is that Warlock will achieve the sort of peaceful equilibrium and balance that the tarot card Temperance represents.

UPRIGHT: You've achieved a healthy balance in your life. Right now, moderation and mildness are the keys to your happiness and success. Beware of extremes and excesses and stay on the straight and narrow path, and you'll continue to thrive.

REVERSED: You're no longer in alignment with your highest self. Reversed, Temperance warns you to prioritize finding balance in your life. If you find yourself overindulging or taking part in harmful vices, this is your call to turn your behavior around. Instant gratification is fleeting. Focus on setting yourself up for long-term success instead.

XV · The Devil

The Devil represents vice, excess, overindulgence, and temptation. Though you may feel as though you're caught in Satan's snare, you actually have more power in this situation than you think.

UPRIGHT: You're battling temptation and vice. While your situation may feel dire, the main message of the Devil card is that you're more in control than you give yourself credit for. Though it's easy to blame the Devil for your predicament, you got yourself into this mess, and you can get yourself out of it. Commit to change, right your wrongs, and free yourself.

REVERSED: Like Adam Young as he stands up to his devilishly devious father to reject the role of antichrist, you're finally finding freedom. Whether you've conquered a vice, harmful habit, or bad situation, a lot of conscious effort and bravery went into overcoming it. You should be very proud of yourself! Take whatever steps are necessary to make sure you're not ensnared in a situation like that again.

XVI · THE TOWER

The Tower represents unexpected catastrophe and devastation. It's as if a swirling vortex of hellfire were to sweep through a pillar in your life.

UPRIGHT: There's no way around it: A central force in your life—something you thought was stable and dependable—has unexpectedly crumbled. It feels as though an all-consuming hellfire has swept through and destroyed something that felt indestructible. Things may seem grim now, but with a little hope and cleverness, you'll come out on top when these cataclysmic trials are over.

REVERSED: Reversed, the Tower shows that you've narrowly avoided a major collapse in your life (whew!). On the other hand, this card can suggest that you're trying your hardest to avoid a collapse that, deep down, you know is inevitable. Change can be frightening and daunting, especially if you can't imagine what your life will look like on the other side of it. Still, you know what has to happen. Avoiding it isn't doing you any good. It's time to let go and start anew.

XVII · THE STAR

The Star, like the angel Aziraphale, is a glowing beacon of hope and goodness. It shines brightly on an otherwise dark, bleak night to renew your spirit.

UPRIGHT: You've recently gone through a difficult chapter in your life, and you are still feeling a bit dog-eared and battered from the experience. The Star is here to remind you to have hope—your future is bright and full of promise. Make yourself a nice cup of hot cocoa, cozy up with a good book, and take a moment to relax after your tribulations. You're turning the page, and you are on the right path.

REVERSED: Reversed, the Star suggests you're feeling hopeless and lost in despair. You've stopped believing in miracles and magic. Things seem dark and bleak, and you've lost faith in the ineffable plan. To get yourself out of this headspace, look inside yourself. Why did you start this journey? What led you here? Reconnect with your original inspiration to give you the motivation to hold your head up high and move forward.

XVIII · THE MOON

The Moon represents trickery and illusions. Things aren't always what they appear to be, as is the case with Adam Young's four-legged sidekick, Dog, a hellhound.

UPRIGHT: The Moon advises you to trust your intuition when evaluating people and situations. It's important that you give your gut feelings more weight than your logical mind now, because the true nature of things is hidden beneath the surface. Be careful not to fall for illusions. Look beyond the surface and go deeper.

REVERSED: Reversed, the Moon shows that you're in a state of anxiety. Are things really as dire as they seem to be, or is your mind playing tricks on you? Not every terrier is a hellhound, and not every hellhound is as evil as it's made out to be. Take a deep breath. Practice some calming self-care and reevaluate this situation when you're no longer in a state of heightened anxiety. You'll see things a lot more clearly then.

XIX · THE SUN

Like The Them happily playing games in Hogback Wood, the Sun represents innocence, joy, and warmth.

UPRIGHT: Hooray! This card calls for a celebration. You're happy, supported, and joyful. What could be better? Take care to stay present and savor this period in time. If this card is drawn in a tarot reading asking about a future outcome, this is a positive sign that you'll be successful and the outcome will be positive.

REVERSED: Just as darkness spreads over Hogback Wood as Adam begins stepping into his power as the antichrist, it may feel like the sunshine has gone out of your life. Though the situation seems bleak, take comfort in knowing that it won't last forever. There's always hope and a silver lining. You'll get through this period of sadness and be on your way to sunnier days.

XX · JUDGMENT

Just as Dagon seeks to invoke punishment for Crowley for disloyalty to his fellow demons, the Judgment card is a call to retribution and eventual absolution.

UPRIGHT: Try as Dagon might to bring Crowley to unholy justice, the plan fails. Crowley puts the fear of God into demonkind and wins absolution due to a miraculous survival that stuns onlookers. Take this card as your call to step into your own power and your own authentic place in the world. Hold your head up high and embrace who you were meant to be, even if your role is unconventional.

REVERSED: Mistakes you've made in the past are causing self-doubt, rendering you unable to level up in life. Do what you need to do to make peace with your past. This is the only way you'll be able to move forward and confidently step into your role in the Divine Plan.

XXI · THE WORLD

The World represents completion and things coming full circle, like the powerful relationship between Aziraphale and Crowley.

UPRIGHT: Congratulations are in order! You've come to the end of an exciting—and sometimes perilous—journey. It may feel as though you've been through both heaven and hell, but you've emerged from the whirlwind a more fulfilled, whole person. Savor the moment but don't get too comfortable; another adventure awaits you as soon as you're ready to embrace it.

REVERSED: You're at the precipice of completion, but some unfinished business is keeping you from fully ending this chapter and beginning a new one. Try as you might to avoid them, know that you can't move forward until all the details are taken care of. Get to it—the world awaits!

MINOR ARCANA

SUIT OF ANGELS

KING OF ANGELS

UPRIGHT: The King of Angels represents a determined, masterful communicator in a position of power—like Metatron, who's also known as the Voice of God. This card advises you to wield your words wisely. Your charm and the way you socialize and interact with others now can give you the power and authority you need to bring your goals to fruition.

REVERSED: Have you been acting impulsively lately? Speaking without considering the potential consequences and true weight of your words will cause others to question your leadership. Stay dedicated to your vision, but don't let your drive and focus blind you to the way your words impact those working toward this goal with you. Otherwise, you might end up with a revolt on your heavenly hands.

QUEEN OF ANGELS

UPRIGHT: Much of the Queen of Angels' power comes from her confidence. Like the archangel Michael, who has the grace and self-assuredness to walk tall even in a dank, dark room full of bloodthirsty demons, the Queen of Angels says what's on her mind with such vision and authority that few dare to question her. This card suggests that it's your time to shine! Embrace your creativity and share your ideas and plans with others. You'll find that they'll be drawn to your self-confidence and conviction.

REVERSED: Right now, you're lacking self-confidence. To regain your signature stride, reconnect with your original vision. What motivates you? What are your aspirations? Create a vision board to overcome this self-confidence slump and rededicate yourself to your goals. You can move heaven and earth if you want to; you just have to believe in your own might.

SUIT OF ANGELS

Knight of Angels

UPRIGHT: The Knight of Angels is focused and action-oriented, like the archangel Uriel. Embrace her sense of no-nonsense ambition and put real action behind your vision for the future. You know what your task is and where you stand in the ineffable plan. It's time to put in the work to manifest your goals in the real world.

REVERSED: Have you been trying to juggle too many tasks at once? You may be scattering your energy and accomplishing very little because of it. Don't be distracted from the main goal. Prioritize your to-do list, delegate some work to others if need be, and stick to the plan.

PAGE OF ANGELS

UPRIGHT: The Page of Angels is an enthusiastic yet inexperienced go-getter. You're eager to start an exciting new role, like Muriel sent to earth on an angelic reconnaissance mission. The trick is to maintain your enthusiasm and commitment to your new directive while not allowing overconfidence to blunder the assignment.

REVERSED: If you're feeling like you're not quite ready to unleash your creativity to the world, the Page of Angels, when reversed, is a call to ask yourself why that is. Are you truly unprepared, or is a lack of confidence stopping you from taking the next step? Don't sabotage your own success by letting fear prevent you from getting started.

ACE OF ANGELS

UPRIGHT: Hallelujah! The Ace of Angels represents a miraculous world of new opportunities revealing itself to you. You're feeling reenergized by all the beautiful possibilities around you. Pursue your creative vision. There's no telling what wonders await if you stay focused on your passion for this new adventure.

REVERSED: Reversed, the Ace of Angels suggests that a new venture isn't going according to plan. You may be experiencing unexpected problems and delays that are making you question whether you should pursue this goal any further. Before you give up, take another look at your plan. Have you clearly defined the steps that need to be taken to achieve success? Or have you been a bit scattered and impulsive in pursuit of your goal? Consider restructuring your path to success and giving your dream another shot.

II OF ANGELS

UPRIGHT: In heaven, Saraqael watches purple plumes rise out of the globe, and each one represents a miracle. Your vision board is made and your goal is set, but it feels like you'd need a miracle to bring your vision to life—a miracle of proportions so great it would light up that heavenly sphere like a brilliant firework. Don't allow yourself to become overwhelmed by the grandiosity of your goal. Just focus on the next steps.

REVERSED: Your motivation has fizzled out. You've lost sight of your goal, and you are feeling aimless. Though you may feel like these are the end times, fear not: They aren't. Remember why you started pursuing this dream. What's at the heart of it? Reconnecting with your vision will give you the get-up-and-go you need to start making progress again.

III of Angels

UPRIGHT: The III of Angels is a card of preparation and expansion. Whether you're preparing your angelic army for an epic battle against demonkind or your goals are a little less cataclysmic, it's clear that the time is right to embrace opportunities that come your way and prepare for the challenges that follow.

REVERSED: Sometimes, in order to grow, we have to step outside of our comfort zones. Aziraphale stands up to the other archangels when he feels Armageddon should be avoided and they're going about things the wrong way. Learn from his example and follow your conscience and heart, even if doing so causes some conflict and discomfort.

IV OF ANGELS

UPRIGHT: The IV of Angels represents milestones and celebrations. Whether you're turning another year older, you're preparing for a reunion, or you've just narrowly managed to save the world from Armageddon, it's clear that a little fête is in order. Take Aziraphael's example by tucking into your favorite celebratory sushi and pour yourself a glass of bubbles. You deserve it.

REVERSED: Reversed, IV of Angels suggests that you're experiencing insecurity on a foundational level. This could mean you're going through a major career shift or moving to a new location, or perhaps you're feeling insecure because Armageddon is on the horizon and the fate of the world rests in the hands of a young boy who happens to be the antichrist. Do what you can to make yourself comfortable during this unsettling transition.

V OF ANGELS

UPRIGHT: Like Uriel and Michael vying to take over while Gabriel is out of commission, you've found yourself locked in a fierce competition. This conflict is creating a lot of chaos and noise. Hold your head up high and fight for the position that's rightfully yours. Creativity will be the key to outwitting your opponent.

REVERSED: While the upright V of Angels represents external conflict, when the card is reversed, that battle becomes internal. Whether you're trying to figure out where you stand on a moral issue or trying to make a tough, complicated decision, it's clear that you're embroiled in inner turmoil. Try to cut through the noise. Make time for serious self-reflection to figure out where you really stand on this issue.

VI of Angels

UPRIGHT: You're feeling on top of the world! You're center stage now, and it's time to soak up the hard-earned applause. You're finally being celebrated for your talents and accomplishments. Take a bow!

REVERSED: Are you trying hard to gain the applause of people who just don't want to give it? The harsh reality is that not everyone will appreciate you the way you deserve to be appreciated. Rather than chasing external validation, be your own cheerleader. If you celebrate yourself, your self-confidence will inspire others.

VII of Angels

UPRIGHT: Your hard work has led to great rewards. However, you can't let your guard down to enjoy them just yet because they're under threat. In the name of all that is good and holy, stand your ground. You may not need a flaming sword, but put your heart and might into protecting what's yours or you may lose everything you've worked for.

REVERSED: You're under a lot of pressure, and it's coming from a powerful force. Though you may feel beaten down and ready to give up, the VII of Angels card, when reversed, urges you to reconnect with your inner power. Remembering who you are and what you're capable of will give you the boost you need to shake the negative forces weighing you down once and for all.

VIII OF ANGELS

UPRIGHT: Life has become so fast-paced that you feel like it's whizzing by. Embrace the momentum! Sometimes this card signifies actual travel. If you go with the flow, you may soon find yourself on an unexpected road trip.

REVERSED: Things are moving uncomfortably quickly, and you're trying in vain to slam on the brakes. Resisting the current pace won't do you any good; opportunities will simply whiz past you if you don't give up a bit of control and let others set the speed. Take comfort in knowing that this action-packed period is only temporary. Life will slow down soon enough.

IX of Angels

UPRIGHT: A battle is being fought. Whether this refers to a momentous war between angels and demons or a more mundane, earthly plight, it's clear that you're feeling exhausted from the effort you've expended. Persevere! The end is in sight.

REVERSED: Do you feel as though you're under attack? Reversed, the IX of Angels asks you to make sure you're seeing the situation at hand clearly. What seems like an intentional affront might simply be a case of miscommunication. Get clarity before starting an avoidable all-out war.

X of Angels

UPRIGHT: This is a very busy time for you, and more tasks, conundrums, and problems to solve are coming your way. Stay on top of your responsibilities. Don't get sidetracked by foodie dreams of crêpes at the Ritz! Keep your focus where it needs to be and you'll be free to sit down with a nice book and mug of hot cocoa in no time.

REVERSED: You're feeling weighed down by a heavy burden, like the moral conundrum Aziraphael faces when confronted with poor Elspeth's grave robbing. Don't sink beneath the weight of this dilemma. Stay focused on the bigger picture to avoid getting bogged down and distracted by the details. Remember, you know in your heart what's right.

SUIT OF VESSELS

KING OF VESSELS

UPRIGHT: Just as Witchfinder Sergeant Shadwell finds himself charmed by the kind Madame Tracy's thoughtfulness and domestic inclinations, the King of Vessels represents emotional nurturing and compassion. Often, this card comes as a call to lead with kindness and stay sensitive to the feelings of others.

REVERSED: When reversed, the King of Vessels becomes manipulative and bossy. He's not above fibbing (or pretending to govern an entire army of witchfinders that doesn't even exist) to get his way. Don't give in to his outbursts and gaslighting; that will only encourage him. The best way to deal with someone like the reversed King of Vessels is to keep a level, logical head.

QUEEN OF VESSELS

UPRIGHT: Like kind and thoughtful Madame Tracy, who brings warm, home-cooked meals to the lonely, eccentric bachelor next door, the Queen of Vessels is sensitive to the emotional needs of those around her. Her intuitive, nurturing presence is always welcome. If you're facing a predicament, this card is a sign to listen to your heart.

REVERSED: When reversed, the Queen of Vessels allows emotions to get the better of her. If you've been struggling to find a calm equilibrium within a wide range of emotional extremes, it's time to pause and take a step back. Consider calling up a neighborly friend like Madame Tracy for a grounding chat and refreshing spot of tea. You'll walk away with a healthy new perspective.

KNIGHT OF VESSELS

UPRIGHT: The Knight of Vessels is a sensitive soul who's eager to please, like Newton Pulsifer. This card represents the heroic, dashing "knight in shining armor" archetype, a role Newton certainly seems to fit as far as Anathema Device is concerned! Take this as a sign to indulge a little. Pamper yourself and practice decadent self-care. You'll come away feeling your best.

REVERSED: Try as he might to make friends, fit in, and succeed professionally, unlucky Newton Pulsifer repeatedly finds himself failing. If you've met with failure recently and you're feeling sulky and sad, remember that tomorrow is a new day. You never know what wonderful adventures (or enchanting witches) are waiting for you on the horizon. Chin up!

MINOR ARCANA

PAGE OF VESSELS

UPRIGHT: The Page of Vessels is someone with a dream in their heart. Just as Maggie, the record shop owner, pines for the barista Nina, the Page of Vessels is a romantic person whose aspirations haven't yet materialized in the real world. Know that your dreams do have potential, even if it seems like it would take divine intervention to make them come true. Hope, wonder, and imagination keep life interesting.

REVERSED: Reversed, the Page of Vessels is keeping their cards close to their chest. You may be formulating plans to make your dreams come true, but you're not yet ready to share your aspirations and schemes with the world. Don't feel pressured to rush the process; take all the time you need. The result will be worth the wait.

ACE OF VESSELS

UPRIGHT: You're feeling creative, artistic, and open to new opportunities for fulfillment and joy. Your effervescence attracts all the right people now. Often, this card indicates a blossoming new love or close friendship. Keep your eyes and heart open!

REVERSED: You've given and given until you've run dry. Reversed, the Ace of Vessels advises you to show yourself the same care and love that you've shown to others in your life. Nurture yourself. After all, you can't pour from an empty vessel! Make time for wholesome self-care to refresh and reinvigorate yourself.

II OF VESSELS

UPRIGHT: The II of Vessels represents a budding partnership. Whether romantic, friendly, or family oriented, this connection has the potential to become powerful and mutually beneficial. You nurture and support each other in ways that allow you both to bloom. There's no telling where this new relationship will take you!

REVERSED: Reversed, II of Vessels indicates a misalignment within an interpersonal connection. Perhaps, like the store owner Maggie, you're pining for someone who's just not emotionally available to give you what you want right now. Is this connection doomed, or is it just a case of bad timing? Perhaps only time will tell.

III of Vessels

UPRIGHT: The III of Vessels encourages you to get together with your closest friends, whether it's for a bike ride, to enjoy ice cream cones, or to play imaginative games at your den in the woods. The ones closest to you bring out the very best in you. Enjoy their company and the rejuvenation and inspiration that comes from spending quality time with them.

REVERSED: You're feeling withdrawn, and that's okay. We all need time to ourselves now and then. If you don't feel like getting together with friends and family now, put your focus on self-care instead. Nurture your own inner world until you feel like joining others again. Read an imaginative book, care for your prized plants (or threaten them into growing better—whatever suits you), or have a crêpe and listen to some bebop. You'll be feeling better and ready to rejoin the world in no time.

IV of Vessels

UPRIGHT: Remember, friend, whether it's offered by an angel or a demon, you're not required to accept every opportunity put before you. Beware impulsivity now; take the time to consider your options carefully before acting.

REVERSED: Aimless and lacking motivation, you've lost touch with your sense of inspiration. "What's the point?" has become your inner mantra, and it's really not serving you well. Time for a change! Making a conscious effort to reconnect with the things you're passionate about will bring back your effervescent spark.

V of Vessels

UPRIGHT: Oh, bugger. You've experienced an unexpected setback, and you may be feeling regretful or remorseful. While this turn of events is unfortunate, know that not all is lost. Take Maggie's example and give yourself a much-needed pep talk! Life is filled with multitudes of miraculous possibilities. Remember the vastness of this situation's potential before you get stuck in the mire of your own disappointment.

REVERSED: You've recently experienced disappointment, and you're sinking into sadness and regret. Oh, dear. Drowning in your own sorrow isn't going to lead to the fulfillment you crave. Stop dwelling on the past. Who knows what wondrous, new opportunities the ineffable plan has in store for you? They may pass you by if you're not receptive to them.

VI OF VESSELS

UPRIGHT: The VI of Vessels invites you to reconnect with the happiness of your past—if you can remember your past, that is. If you're feeling a little lost and homesick like the archangel Gabriel, get together with an old friend. Reminiscing with a trusted friend over a cup of hot cocoa will do you a world of good.

REVERSED: Reversed, the VI of Vessels suggests that you've become preoccupied with the past. Daydreaming about the adventure of days gone by is fine once in a while, but be careful to stay grounded in the present. There are more adventures waiting for you, and you need to be facing forward to greet them. Don't let a fixation with your past inhibit the magic of your future.

VII OF VESSELS

UPRIGHT: You're being met with a litany of dazzling options, but which to choose? Beware of demons in angels' clothing. Don't be fooled by sweet-talking snakes or promises that sound too divine to be true. Take care to see the options for what they truly are before making any final decisions.

REVERSED: Are you feeling overwhelmed by the options before you? You have a choice to make, but you're so afraid of choosing incorrectly that you have stalled and aren't choosing at all. Honestly, delaying further is a poor choice in itself. You've done your research and thought this through. Now close your eyes, say one last prayer, and take the next step.

VIII OF VESSELS

UPRIGHT: Oh, dear. You're experiencing disappointment. Did an angel in your life turn out to be a demon in disguise? The truth is that some connections just aren't meant to last forever. Don't bury your sorrow inside. Allow yourself to really feel your feelings so you can move on from them fully when your tears have dried.

REVERSED: You've found yourself in an emotional conundrum. You may be struggling to decide whether to try reviving a strained personal connection or wash your hands of it and walk away. Be honest with yourself. Deep down, you know what your next step should be.

IX of Vessels

UPRIGHT: Ah, bliss! You're feeling absolutely tickety-boo, emotionally fulfilled and content as can be. Your close connections are nurturing and supportive. Take care to thank them for the value they add to your life. Some would move heaven and earth for you, so let them know how much you appreciate their dedication and support.

REVERSED: During Anathema Device's quest to use Agnes Nutter's prophecies to find the antichrist and prevent Armageddon, she discovers that things aren't always as straightforward as they seem. Just as she ends up befriending the antichrist and falling in love with a witchfinder, you'll find emotional fulfillment in unexpected places. Branch out and make new connections.

X OF VESSELS

UPRIGHT: Congratulations! Hallelujah! Your prayers are being answered. Whether you've hoped and prayed for an idyllic, perfect paradise of a home, true love, or something more mundane, the X of Vessels card represents a wonderfully favorable outcome. Rejoice and enjoy!

REVERSED: Has a personal connection recently soured? You may be feeling a disconnect within an interpersonal dynamic you once revered. If you feel like you're being kicked out of the Garden of Eden, reexamine your own part in this relationship. Have you been swayed by any snakes? Indulged in any forbidden fruit lately? Make sure you're acting in accordance with your own morals and ethics.

SUIT OF DEMONS

KING OF DEMONS

UPRIGHT: Like Beelzebub, leader of the forces of hell, the King of Demons is a focused, fierce, decisive leader who can come across as cold and calculating. This figure leads with *brainzzz* and might, and *advizzzezzz* you to use logic when making decisions.

REVERSED: Has your goal become all-consuming? Reversed, the King of Demons takes ruthlessness to a whole new level. If you've been acting in harsh, Machiavellian ways to achieve your ambitions, this card is a sign to step back to get a healthier perspective on the situation. Don't *bulldozzze* your allies to get what you want.

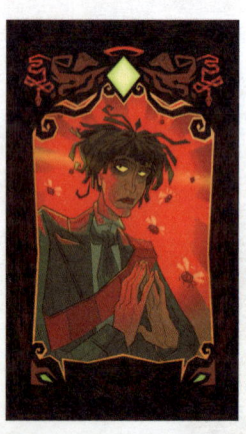

QUEEN OF DEMONS

UPRIGHT: Like the confident, cool, collected, sword-wielding steel horseman of the apocalypse war, the Queen of Demons is a no-nonsense figure whose straightforwardness intimidates others. This card suggests that you channel that blunt energy while navigating connections and decisions now.

REVERSED: Reversed, the Queen of Demons suggests that your emotions have taken over, and you may be acting in manipulative, cold-hearted ways as a result. It's time to get your feelings under control. Don't impulsively burn bridges you may one day need.

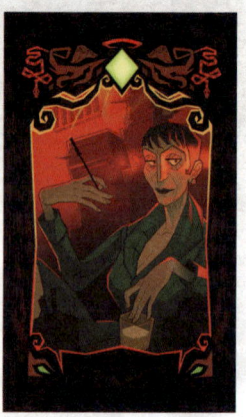

KNIGHT OF DEMONS

UPRIGHT: The Knight of Demons is a focused, action-oriented, ambitious person like the impeccably dressed hell-maven Shax. This card warns you not to let anything distract you from actively pursuing your goal now. Don't allow others to sweet talk you, and don't get caught up in the chaos around you. Follow through with your plan with single-minded focus.

REVERSED: Your ambition has driven you to chaotic impulsivity, and your lack of calculation and forethought has foiled your plans. To correct this misstep, you'll need to dust yourself off and come up with a strategic, actionable plan.

PAGE OF DEMONS

UPRIGHT: This card represents characteristics of the bumbling, brain-hungry booksellers Harmony and Glozier or military officer Greta Kleinschmidt: ambitious and eager to further their cause but unable to pull off a dastardly plan successfully. Beware of overconfidence; a lack of experience may be to blame for missteps now.

REVERSED: No one likes a know-it-all—particularly when they clearly don't know it all. Talk is cheap, and people can see through overconfident posturing better than you think. Be honest about your skill set and be willing to learn. Admitting that you don't know everything isn't the sign of weakness you think it is.

ACE OF DEMONS

UPRIGHT: At last! This is your eureka moment! Embrace this breakthrough by having a major brainstorming session. Jot down all your brilliant, visionary ideas. You're in an exciting whirlwind of mental power and potential. Make the most of it!

REVERSED: The Ace of Demons suggests that a plan hasn't developed the way you hoped it would. It's time to scrap this idea and go back to the beginning. Don't let this discourage you; your goal is still attainable! You just need to rethink your plan and start over with a brand-new strategy.

II of Demons

UPRIGHT: The II of Demons represents a difficult decision to be made. Crowley faces a similar conundrum about how to proceed when his enemy, Gabriel, turns up at Aziraphael's bookshop, vulnerable and in need of help. At this moment, you don't have the clarity and information you need to make the best choice. Hunt down the facts and do the necessary calculations to come up with the most logical move forward.

REVERSED: You have a decision to make but cannot for the life of you decide what to do. This delay isn't helping the matter. Sometimes indecision can have greater consequences than a poor decision. Flip a coin if you have to. It's time to make up your mind.

III of Demons

UPRIGHT: It's an unfortunate fact that even the best-laid ineffable plans fall through sometimes. Though you're feeling betrayed and disappointed, this heartbreak won't last forever. Give yourself the time you need to grieve this loss.

REVERSED: A recent disappointment or loss has felt all-consuming in your life lately, but you're finally turning a corner in your grief. Healing comes from allowing yourself to feel and express what you need to. Say what you need to say, and then take the first steps forward.

IV of Demons

UPRIGHT: The IV of Demons advises you to kick up your feet and relax! Luxuriate in a warm bath, or perhaps indulge in a moisturizing face mask. A fierce battle lies ahead, and you need to do everything in your power to make sure you're rejuvenated and ready for what's to come.

REVERSED: You've been so busy lately! Have self-care and relaxation fallen by the wayside as a result? You can't go on like this forever. A period of rest and peace is absolutely required now to overcome your exhaustion. Take a break and you'll be feeling fighting-fit again in no time.

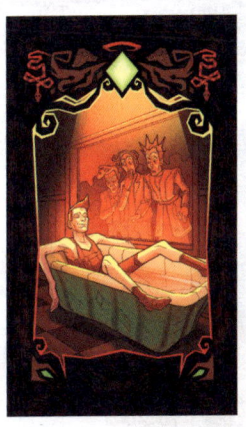

V of Demons

UPRIGHT: The V of Demons represents battles, conflicts, and war . . . but is all of this really necessary? Perhaps angels and demons are too evenly matched, and no good or progress will come of this. If there's to be no winning in this situation, swallow your pride and strike a truce.

REVERSED: You've been embroiled in conflict recently, and you're ready to pick up the pieces of the war zone. No matter who won, there are no real winners. Lick your wounds, salvage what you can, and move on.

VI of Demons

UPRIGHT: The VI of Demons card denotes some sort of shift or transition. Whether you're experiencing a major change in your mindset or ethics or it's your turn to step up to one of the New Resident reception desks in hell, it's clear that this will be a transformative experience in your world. This current metamorphosis and the decisions you make during the change will lay the groundwork for your future.

REVERSED: Change can be uncomfortable. We all know this! However, holding fast to what's comfortable doesn't make for much personal growth. It's time for you to embrace new ideas and move forward in life.

VII of Demons

UPRIGHT: Have you been prioritizing other people's needs and wants at the expense of your own? If you're feeling burned out and overwhelmed, the VII of Demons card advises you to put your foot down and make your own interests a priority for once.

REVERSED: Self-doubt and imposter syndrome are eating away at you. That is just anxiety and fear talking! Take control by reminding yourself how strong and capable you actually are. You've got what it takes to win this war!

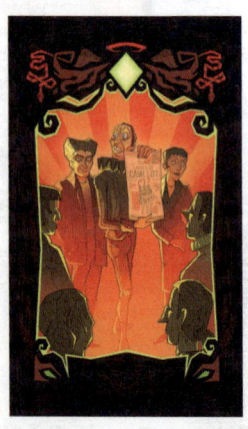

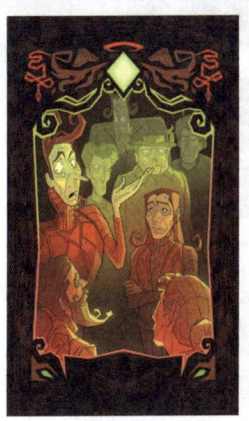

VIII of Demons

UPRIGHT: Your situation feels dire, but are you truly as stuck as you think you are? The VIII of Demons suggests that your perception of this predicament is holding you back more than the predicament itself. A new perspective will set you free.

REVERSED: The VIII of Demons suggests that if the atmosphere feels hellish, a negative mindset may be to blame. It may feel like you've lost the war, but in reality, things haven't even started. Take some time to relax and rejuvenate yourself mentally so you're fully prepared to meet what's to come head-on.

IX of Demons

UPRIGHT: Anxiety and worry are looming large in your life at the moment, but you haven't fallen over the edge into despair and paranoia just yet. Prioritize regaining a better perspective. Perhaps ice cream cones with friends and a relaxing walk through Hogback Wood is in order?

REVERSED: Don't believe everything you read—or think. Is the world really coming to an end? Are everyone and everything truly filled with nefarious motives, or is your mind just pushing away your sense of balance and logic? Don't allow illogical fears to take over your life.

X of Demons

UPRIGHT: Do you feel as though you've been stabbed in the back? The X of Demons represents painful, unexpected twists of fate. Though you may feel heartbroken and betrayed now, rest assured that this event will make room for better connections and opportunities than the ones that have been destroyed.

REVERSED: Refusing to acknowledge the truth of a situation doesn't make that truth any less real or important. A connection, ambition, or dream in your life needs to come to an end, but you're still clinging to it long after you should have let go. It's time.

SUIT OF HUMANS

KING OF HUMANS

UPRIGHT: Rejoice! The King of Humans represents success and abundance. Like Job, you've created a lasting legacy of comfort for your family. You've worked hard to cultivate material wealth and stability. It's time to enjoy the fruit of your efforts.

REVERSED: Reversed, the King of Humans suggests you might be mishandling your material wealth or assets. Are you spending more than you're bringing in? Perhaps you're hoarding enough gold to make the angels themselves jealous. Examine the way you're spending and saving money—a better balance needs to be created.

MINOR ARCANA

Queen of Humans

UPRIGHT: Like Anathema Device, you want for nothing. While your wealth may not have been passed down like the wisdom of a seventeenth-century prophetic ancestor, it's clear that you're living the good life. You take care of your responsibilities while also prioritizing self-care and comfort. Sometimes you really can have it all!

REVERSED: Reflect on how you're distributing your energy. Are you focused on work to the point that your home life is a bit neglected? Perhaps family has taken center stage in your life so that your other commitments have fallen by the wayside. It's time to strike a better balance.

KNIGHT OF HUMANS

UPRIGHT: Like Mrs. Henderson, the hardworking, no-nonsense impresario of the Windmill, you are focused, skilled, and following through with your tasks. Others appreciate your work ethic and commitment. Keep it up!

REVERSED: Reversed, the Knight of Humans suggests that you're lacking motivation. You're having trouble finishing what you start and fully honoring your commitments and responsibilities. Mrs. Henderson wouldn't stand for that! Reversed, this card is a wake-up call to reignite your momentum and start making real, tangible progress again.

PAGE OF HUMANS

UPRIGHT: The Page of Humans represents an entrepreneurial spirit, like poor Elspeth. She does what she has to do to survive, even if the job (grave robbing!) is unpleasant and rather dangerous. This card advises you to take note of the moneymaking opportunities all around you now. Sometimes the unconventional offers pay off the most.

REVERSED: You're letting your imposter syndrome prevent you from reaching your full potential. Is anyone really ever fully prepared to take the next step? You don't need to have all the answers now. Sometimes you just have to pull yourself up by the bootstraps like Elspeth, be brave, and do what you have to do to move forward.

ACE OF HUMANS

UPRIGHT: The Ace of Humans represents exciting new opportunities for financial and material success. Out of the ashes of a failed venture (or convent burned down by a callous demon), something new can rise. Take the example of Sister Mary Loquacious and look for unexpected opportunities for entrepreneurialism.

REVERSED: Reversed, the Ace of Humans advises caution. Perhaps a new business venture isn't going according to plan, or someone oversold you on an investment and is now under-delivering. Don't act impulsively where money and finances are concerned. Make sure you have all the facts, figures, and details before moving forward with new jobs or finance-related partnerships.

II of Humans

UPRIGHT: The II of Humans is all about work-life balance. It can be difficult to make sure your family and home are getting as much attention as they need while still fulfilling responsibilities at work, as U.S. Ambassador Thaddeus Dowling can attest. Prioritize maintaining a healthy balance of work and play.

REVERSED: Reversed, this card suggests that your work-life balance has gone out the window. You're feeling overwhelmed and overcommitted, and other areas of your life are being neglected because of it. It's clear that the way you're spending your time and energy needs an overhaul.

III OF HUMANS

UPRIGHT: The III of Humans represents collaboration and synergy. You're coming together with others to create something special (and lucrative!). This new venture has the potential for major success. Make sure the work is divided fairly and the expectations are clearly defined.

REVERSED: Alas, things haven't gone according to plan. A collaborative effort in your life has devolved into chaos, like Madame Tracy's séance. Bringing focus back to the original goal will help get everyone back on track.

IV of Humans

UPRIGHT: You're working hard to create stability in your finances and home life. While this is an excellent and important goal, be careful not to become too selfish or miserly in the process.

REVERSED: Have you been sticking to your budget? Have you paid all your expenses before indulging in frivolous purchases? Reversed, the IV of Humans asks you to evaluate how you're spending money. The opportunity exists for you to make better choices.

V OF HUMANS

UPRIGHT: Life is tough right now. Whether you've lost your job or an unexpected expense has put you in a bad financial position, it's clear that things are hard, and you're having trouble seeing how to get yourself out of this. Remember that you deserve comfort, safety, and happiness. Keep going.

REVERSED: Hallelujah! You've been through a financially rough period recently, but things are finally stabilizing for you. At some points, you couldn't see a way out of your hardship, so this feels like a bona fide miracle! Keep your eyes peeled for the new opportunities that are coming your way.

VI of Humans

UPRIGHT: The VI of Humans advises you to remember your humanity. Give to those less fortunate if you're in a position to do so. If you're struggling, don't be timid about asking for help. Life can be hard; everyone needs a helping hand now and then.

REVERSED: Reversed, the VI of Humans suggests that you've been as dedicated to your tasks as the International Express man, Leslie. It's time for a break! You've gone to the ends of the earth to fulfill your responsibilities, and you can afford to relax a little. You've earned it!

VII of Humans

UPRIGHT: Hard work and dedication set you up for long-term success in the future. Like the entrepreneurial Maggie, you're passionate about your job. The message of the VII of Humans card is to keep working toward your goals because you're well on your way to achieving them.

REVERSED: Maggie considers closing her record shop due to a lack of customers, and this card suggests you're having similar feelings about throwing in the towel. You're discouraged by a lack of immediate success. Only you know whether it's time to cut your losses, but make sure your expectations are realistic before deciding to give up completely.

VIII of Humans

UPRIGHT: Repetitive tasks (like cutting out potential leads from a massive stack of Witchfinder Sergeant Shadwell's newspapers) might be boring, but those are the dues you have to pay to achieve success in the future. Stick to your assignment and you'll reach your goals before you know it!

REVERSED: Reversed, the VIII of Humans suggests that you're getting bogged down in details at the expense of your overall mission. Don't allow little snags to distract you from making progress on the bigger picture.

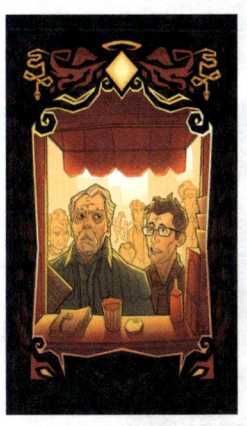

IX of Humans

UPRIGHT: The IX of Humans card invites you to live a little! Like Neighborhood Watch founder R. P. Tyler, you've worked hard, stayed vigilant, and done your duty admirably. Take a break to enjoy the comforts your long-term efforts have provided you with, and have some fun!

REVERSED: It's time to reevaluate your own worth. Don't sell yourself short! The skills, services, and knowledge you have to offer are valuable. The IX of Humans, when reversed, suggests that this isn't the time for modesty. Don't settle for less than you deserve.

X of Humans

UPRIGHT: Agnes Nutter's descendants are so dedicated to her nice and extremely accurate prophecies and advice that they've created massive amounts of wealth and abundance for themselves. The X of Humans card invites you to notice the comfort, stability, and abundance all around you, and express gratitude for it.

REVERSED: Reversed, the X of Humans suggests that you have everything you set out to manifest in your life, but achieving your material goals hasn't made you as happy as you thought it would. Have you been defining success by someone else's measure? Some introspection will help you discover what you truly need to feel fulfilled.

SUIT OF HUMANS

TAROT READINGS

One of the most wonderful things about tarot reading is that the experience can easily be personalized to suit your personality, mood, and style. Feel free to use tarot intuitively, in whatever way feels right to you. You can read tarot as often or infrequently as you like. Make it a sacred ritual performed by candlelight or take out your deck casually in a coffee shop for readings with friends. How you read tarot is all up to you! That's the splendor of it.

CARING FOR YOUR DECK

Most tarot readers agree that it's important to energetically cleanse your deck regularly, especially if you use it to read tarot for other people. Cleansing your deck leaves you with a clean slate so your next tarot session will be fresh, clear, and unencumbered by the energy of previous readings.

There are many methods you can use to cleanse your tarot deck, so feel free to experiment with them to find the one that resonates with you. Smoke cleansing, for example, involves passing the tarot deck through the smoke of sacred, smoldering herbs, such as sage, lavender, or palo santo. Placing your deck in the moonlight overnight can cleanse and refresh your cards, too. Many agree that the light of a full moon is the most powerful, but any moonlight will do the job. Another option is to use crystals; selenite, in particular, is a wonderful cleansing tool. Keep selenite sticks or spheres atop your deck when it's not in use to make sure it's ready for the next reading. Some readers place their tarot decks in boxes made of selenite or keep them resting on selenite slabs.

PREPARING TO READ TAROT

Begin your tarot reading by formulating a clear question for the cards. You can ask them anything and everything: *Will Nina and I ever be a romantic item? How can I stop Armageddon and save the world? Am I doomed to be a poor grave robber for all time? What's my role in God's ineffable plan?* Tarot can give you useful insight and advice about any situation you may find yourself in.

Begin tarot readings by relaxing and clearing your head. Meditate, take a relaxing bath, or just close your eyes for a few moments. When you're ready, ask your question and shuffle the tarot deck. Some people shuffle the cards like playing cards, while others use an overhand shuffle to avoid bending them. You can even spread them out facedown on a large surface and rifle through them to select cards intuitively.

When your question has been asked and your cards have been shuffled, it's time to draw cards and lay them out in a tarot spread. Tarot spreads are the specific ways cards are arranged as they're drawn. Here are a few spreads to help you get started.

THE SPREADS

THE INEFFABLE PLAN

Are you feeling a little lost? Has Crowley tempted you from the straight and narrow path? Have you put so much effort into doing everything by the book that you're feeling a bit stagnant or bored? Perhaps you're wondering what your next steps forward should look like. If you're having trouble understanding your role in the Great Plan of life, this tarot spread will help you find clarity about your future.

1. *What's my current position in the great ineffable plan?* This tarot card represents your position right now. It reveals the defining aspect of this current phase in your life.

2. *What's holding me back?* This tarot card reveals what you need to let go of and leave behind as you move into the future.

3. *What will propel me forward?* This tarot card reveals what you need to hold on to and bring with you into the future.

4. *What will my next life chapter look like?* This tarot card represents the defining feature of the next phase in your life.

5. *What advice do you have for me as I transition into the future?* This tarot card offers final advice to keep in mind while transitioning into the next chapter of your life.

THE DOCTOR'S QUANDARY

As Aziraphale learns from the moral conundrum associated with Elspeth's grave digging, things aren't always black and white. The world isn't neatly divided into *good* and *evil*. Sometimes situations call for nuanced thought and careful consideration before judgment can be passed on them. This tarot spread is designed to help you work through dilemmas in your life.

1. *What's at the heart of this problem?* This tarot card represents the true nature of the dilemma in question.

2. *What's the shadow side of this situation?* This tarot card reveals the shadow side of this predicament and how the situation may be harmful.

3. *What's the light in this situation?* This tarot card shows how the situation may be beneficial or positive.

4. *What's the most important thing to keep in mind when making this decision?* This tarot card offers final advice to help you come to the best possible conclusion.

THE SPREADS

Gabriel's Self-Discovery

It turns out that feeling a little lost isn't relegated solely to the human condition. Even angels need help reconnecting with their truest selves every now and again. If you're feeling out of alignment, this tarot spread will help you remember who you really are and allow you to reconnect with your authentic self.

1. *What's my best personality trait?* This tarot card reveals the trait you need to hold on to and celebrate.

2. *What behavior pattern or aspect of my personality could use improvement?* This tarot card reveals what you need to work on.

3. *How can I be a better friend to others?* This tarot card shows how you can show up for others in a more authentic, supportive way.

4. *What baggage from the past should I let go of?* This tarot card reveals something from your past that needs to stay there so you can move forward freely into your future.

5. *What aspect of life do I need to focus on to find true fulfillment?* This tarot card reveals where you'll find true happiness and fulfillment on a deep, personal level.

THE SPREADS

ABOUT THE AUTHOR

Minerva Siegel is a writer, author, sensitivity reader, tarot consultant, and longtime practitioner of witchcraft who haunts a Victorian home in Milwaukee, Wisconsin, with her gruff Taurean double-Virgo husband and their motley pack of rescue dogs. In addition to this book, she's the author of *Tarot for Self-Care: How to Use Tarot to Manifest Your Best Self* and *Spell Jars for the Modern Witch: A Practical Guide to Crafting Spell Jars for Abundance, Luck, Protection, and More*, as well as a dozen licensed tarot decks. Minerva is a disabled wheelchair user. Though the physical body has limitations, there's freedom and power in fully tapping into our own magickal potential. Her many guidebooks help readers do just that. You can find her on Instagram @Author.Minerva.Siegel.

ABOUT THE ILLUSTRATOR

Lúthien Leerghast, known also as Jabberwick, is a queer, self-taught illustrator from Tasmania, Australia. Often depicting fantastical creatures inspired by stop motion animation & puppetry, their work is crooked, whiskered and cunning: an appreciation for that which scuttles at the bottom of the well.

TITAN
BOOKS

A division of Titan Publishing Group Ltd
144 Southwark Street
London SE1 0UP
www.titanbooks.com

f Find us on Facebook: www.facebook.com/TitanBooks
X Follow us on X @titanbooks

© 2023 Amazon Content Services LLC. Good Omens
© 2023 Amazon Content Services LLC.

Published by Titan Books, London, in 2023.

No part of this publication may be reproduced, stored in a retrieval system, or transmitted, in any form or by any means without the prior written permission of the publisher, nor be otherwise circulated in any form of binding or cover other than that in which it is published and without a similar condition being imposed on the subsequent purchaser.

A CIP catalogue record for this title is available from the British Library.

ISBN: 9781803367231

Insight Editions, in association with Roots of Peace, will plant two trees for each tree used in the manufacturing of this book. Roots of Peace is an internationally renowned humanitarian organization dedicated to eradicating land mines worldwide and converting war-torn lands into productive farms and wildlife habitats. Roots of Peace will plant two million fruit and nut trees in Afghanistan and provide farmers there with the skills and support necessary for sustainable land use.

Manufactured in China
10 9 8 7 6 5 4 3